TEN AMERICAN POETS

Ten American Poets is an anthology introducing to a British audience the work of some younger American writers. Most of the poems in the anthology have appeared in American periodicals, including *Poetry* and *New American Review*. The editor, James Atlas, was President of the *Harvard Advocate* and is at present a Rhodes Scholar at New College, Oxford.

In his introduction he describes the conditions under which the contemporary American poet has to work and explains his criteria for selection. The predominance of formal poetry in the anthology and the commitment of all the poets included to their social and literary context, with—at the same time—a wide variety of idioms, themes, and forms, testifies to the vigour and resourcefulness of a new generation of writers responding to new conditions but still finding energy and continuity in the 'main line' of American poetry.

TEN
AMERICAN
POETS

– an anthology of poems by
Alan Williamson, Jonathan Galassi,
Paul Smyth, Peggy Rizza, James Martin,
Richard Tillinghast, Robert B. Shaw,
Jane Shore, Frank Bidart & John Koethe

edited by
James Atlas

A CARCANET PRESS PUBLICATION

Some of these poems have appeared in periodicals, to whose editors acknowledgement is due.

Alan Williamson: *Virginia Quarterly Review*, Winter, 1972, for 'War in the Valley of Vision: Christmas 1967'; *Yale Review* for 'The Hotel with a View of the Jungfrau' Yale © University; *Shenandoah* for 'Van Gogh's Asylum' © 1970 by *Shenandoah*, with permission of the editor.

Paul Smyth: *The Lyric* for 'Trespass'.

Peggy Rizza: *Chicago Review* for 'Water Crossing, Late Afternoon' and 'Dream of Swimming'.

James Martin: *New American Review* for 'A Reunion', 'Pastor Bonhoeffer Becomes Engaged', ' "Your Führer is not AntiChrist" ', 'Pastor Bonhoeffer's Last Prayer, On The Importance of Illusion'; *Esquire* for 'Pastor Bonhoeffer Talks About Hitler'.

Richard Tillinghast: Wesleyan University Press, © 1967, 1968, 1969, by Richard Tillinghast, for 'Until', 'Winter Insomnia', 'The End of Summer in the North', reprinted from *Sleep Watch*, by permission of Wesleyan University Press.

Robert B. Shaw: Anvil Press for 'The Pause'.

Jane Shore: *Audience* for 'Mud Season: Vermont'.

Frank Bidart: George Braziller, © 1973, for 'To My Father', 'Self-Portrait, 1969' 'Herbert White'.

John Koethe: *Quarterly Review of Literature*, Volume XV, numbers 1/2 for 'Bird'; *Audit* for 'The Friendly Animals'.

The following poems first appeared in *Poetry*, and are reprinted by permission of the Editor of *Poetry*: John Koethe, 'Satie's Suits', © 1969; Alan Williamson, 'April 5, 1968' and John Koethe, 'Domes', © 1970; Jonathan Galassi, 'King Caesar's Windows' and Robert B. Shaw, 'Janus' and 'There', © 1971; Paul Smyth, 'Of His Affliction', Robert B. Shaw, 'Another Day', and Jane Shore, 'Ararat' and 'Landing Off Season', © 1972, by The Modern Poetry Association.

SBN 85635 048 6—cloth
SBN 85635 049 4—paper

First Edition Published 1973
by Carcanet Press Limited
266 Councillor Lane
Cheadle Hulme, Cheadle
Cheshire SK8 5PN

Printed in Great Britain by W & J Mackay Limited, Chatham

CONTENTS

ALAN WILLIAMSON was born in Chicago in 1944. Educated at Haverford and Harvard, he has been, since 1969, Assistant Professor of English at the University of Virginia. He is now at work on a book about the political poetry of Robert Lowell.

JONATHAN GALASSI was born in Seattle in 1949 and graduated from Harvard, where he was President of the *Harvard Advocate*. He won a Marshall Scholarship to study English at Christ's College, Cambridge, during 1971–3.

PAUL SMYTH was born in 1944, and grew up in Holliston, Massachusetts. He received his B.A. from Harvard, and has since 1969 been a member of the English Department at Mount Holyoke College. He was awarded *Poetry*'s Dillon Prize for 1971.

PEGGY RIZZA graduated from Radcliffe in 1971, where she had studied under Elizabeth Bishop and Robert Lowell. She is working towards a degree at the Harvard Divinity School.

JAMES MARTIN was born in 1948, and graduated from Colby College in 1970. He is now working towards a Master's degree in theology from Boston University. In 1972, he received the New York Poetry Center's Discovery Award.

RICHARD TILLINGHAST was born in Tennessee in 1940, and attended college at the University of the South, where he was an editorial assistant of *Sewanee Review*. Later on, he taught at Harvard, and is now Assistant Professor of English at Berkeley. His first book, *Sleep Watch*, was published by Wesleyan in 1969.

ROBERT B. SHAW was President of the *Harvard Advocate* while an undergraduate. He is at present a doctoral candidate in English at Yale, and reviews regularly for *Poetry*. A pamphlet of his poems was published by Carcanet Press in 1970, and a further collection by Anvil Press in 1972.

JANE SHORE graduated from Goddard College in 1969, and attended the Iowa Writers' Conference until 1971. She now holds the Briggs-Copland Teaching Fellowship at Harvard.

FRANK BIDART was born in 1939. He received a B.A. from the University of California, and did graduate work at Harvard. He teaches English now at Wellesley. His first book of poems, *Golden State*, is to be published by Braziller in 1973.

JOHN KOETHE was an undergraduate at Princeton, and is now a graduate student in philosophy at Harvard. He was at one time the Boston correspondent for *Art News*, and his poems have appeared in the anthology *Another World*, published by Bobbs-Merrill. His first book of poems, *Domes*, has received the Frank O'Hara Award and is published by Columbia University Press.

INTRODUCTION

IN THE United States, where the cultural tradition remains eva-
nescent (if it exists at all), a dispute about the relation between artists
and the social conditions which surround them has been sustained
over the decades. This question should be raised in any discussion of
the works of art which a society produces; but in our time such re-
lations have become more intricate than ever, their comprehension
more crucial. Because our modern poetic inheritance, even our lan-
guage, is owed to Europe (a tradition which Pound and Eliot
secured), because poets here experience a division between their
discourse and the discourse which is in wider public use, as well as
between their individual mode of production and the productive re-
lations dominant now, the practice of literature in the United States
has been excluded from the nation's life.

Delmore Schwartz expressed this dilemma when he wrote of 'the
isolation of modern poetry'. The poet had become estranged from
the world because the world was no longer susceptible to what could
be called imaginative reference; in other words, it possessed proper-
ties which science could elicit, and so usurp literature's hermeneutical
domain. Schwartz's other observation was that advanced (or late)
industrial society promoted its own 'autonomous satisfactions';
thus, 'it was not so much the poet as it was poetry, culture, sensi-
bility, imagination, that were isolated.' The work of art, then, is
created with instruments which only a limited number of artisans
know how to use.

These contradictions are apparent in all Modernist literature, and
even earlier, in the Romantics' enterprise; Surrealism, German Ex-
pressionist verse, and the anti-aesthetics of Russian Futurism repre-
sent rebellions against a cultural order which couldn't sustain them.
In America, the crisis has become even more explicit, in that no such
order is visible, and one has had to be invented. Eliot's well-known
conviction that 'what happens when a new work of art is created is
something that happens simultaneously to all the works of art which
preceded it' appears to be untenable in a situation where the historical
conditions which shaped the past are no longer evident.

This is what has happened to American poets writing now: un-
able to detect a coherent poetic tradition in their own experience,

9

and aware that their sensibilities reflect a radical separation from the landscape of our time, they have been required to excavate their own sensations and place them at the centre of their work. This doesn't mean that our literature has resurrected that obsession with the mind's operation so reverberant in English Romanticism; rather, it has been obliged to restore its own value, ever since this value lost what it once possessed: confirmation as a valid social activity. And in order to explain this loss, our writers have had to revolutionise poetic technique, to discover a language capable of negation, a language which could refuse this event without abolishing itself.[1]

What options were available? To the poets of the so-called 'Tragic Generation', Robert Lowell, John Berryman, Delmore Schwartz and Randall Jarrell (Sylvia Plath and Theodore Roethke should be named as well), the English tradition still housed unlimited possibilities, even though their own disrupted lives were shown to be rather incompatible with their erudition. During the decades after World War II, when the nation, in Lowell's words, had summoned Ike, 'the mausoleum in her heart', our land was shrouded in the illusion of well-being; these poets, though, could see that the shroud was a mourning-veil. Such revelations as Lowell's were hostile to this 'tranquillised' era, just as the era was hostile to those who divined its temporariness. So there was a logic in resorting to those poetic modes which had in other epochs identified poets as political and public men. It restored to them their proper historical importance, and imbued their poems with an authority that reference and echo serve to promote. Despite this tactic, they resembled Lowell as a child:

> Unseen and all-seeing, I was Agrippina
> in the Golden House of Nero . . .

And it was this contradiction which exacerbated their nerves, and was responsible for the critical epithet, 'Extremist art'.

[1] This has been the case with the Black Mountain poets, who have an immense influence in America. Theirs is a spare and rigorous mode in which the poem threatens to disappear, or else dissolves into sheer demonstration; this, and the revival of irrational associations and motifs, appear to derive from Surrealism, though, as Frederic Jameson has noted, in America 'the objects of Surrealism are gone without a trace'. Because the manner in which commodities have come to be produced is veiled, these poetic experiments, in which such commodities, the objects of our post-industrial world, are celebrated and chronicled, enact their own impoverishment: the text is robbed of content.

THE POETS collected here have all sensed, in some measure, that what was oppressive to their teachers (and several have studied under Lowell) is even more so now, though the formal solutions posed in texts like *Notebook*, the *Dream Songs*, and Jarrell's meditative soliloquies still seem possible to them. What worsens their situation is that the American language has been eroded through exploitative use (in our Administration's discussion of the Vietnam War, in the proliferation of so-called 'popular literature'), while serious writers are dispersed, their work published either in the small academic journals or thrown in competition for space in wide-circulation monthlies. The choices before them, then, have been to form geographical coteries, to publish their own writing themselves, or to teach.

The ten poets represented in these pages lean toward the last-mentioned; their bias is academic, and, to be more specific, all have been associated with Cambridge or Harvard, and with such teachers there as Lowell, Elizabeth Bishop, and Robert Fitzgerald. Several are still students. What has informed their work, above all, is the conviction that a poem's formal qualities determine its authority, and that this authority is required if the poem hopes to claim our attention; otherwise, it succumbs to what George Steiner has called 'ontological derivativeness', the tendency to mirror in a work those properties which exist in lived experience: in our own time, chaos, irrational images (on our TV screens, commercials and Vietnam newsreels are juxtaposed), and linguistic disorder (the various vocabularies and idioms which have arisen in the absence of a received tradition).

While it's obvious that poetry is enriched through these diverse 'language-events', there have been damages as well; if literature appropriates the language now in use, it stipulates its own disappearance. However, if it revives a mode which is archaic, no longer expressive of real conditions, no longer 'the real language of men' spoken in this historical moment, then it abdicates all value. To write in a diction which echoes, imitates, and borrows, even as it reflects the cadences and mannerisms of contemporary speech, is to draw on whatever resources are available now, to evade the limits which restrict Projectivism, American Surrealism, and the New York School.

Alan Williamson's poem, 'War in the Valley of Vision: Christmas 1967' enacts the possibilities I've considered above; Lowellian in its controlled, subdued rhetoric, the poem concentrates on the lurid emblems of what history has become: a lapse from grace, a descent from those religious tropes which once illuminated the world. God's presence is revealed to us through technological devices, 'an on-off bulb'. Like the Baal Shem Tov, we've been denied our inheritance, nothing remains except the traces of wisdom, a blurred remembrance: this explains the *New Testament in Crossword Puzzles* and the Blake quotation. Then there is the bleak intrusion of idiom, the woman whose words emptiness and repetition have spoiled; their significance could even be called archaeological, in that Williamson has unearthed these phrases from the ruins of common speech, and invested them with meaning. This is how 'breakthrough' receives a polemical character; dislocated, in Eliot's sense, from its usual purpose, which is to create among intellectuals an illusion of social change, the word appears in the poem unmasked.

Such disruptions dominate Frank Bidart's 'Herbert White', where the poet's own psychic traumas enable him to devise a language which articulates actual violence; in Jonathan Galassi's colloquial narratives, 'Regression' and 'The Impossibility of Going North', where the voice relates a vision of social disintegration as if it were some natural event; and in Richard Tillinghast's 'Poem Against History', where quotations which once justified America's policies towards the Indian are inscribed in the poem to render more vivid historical truth.

Of course, there are variations on this mode, such as the formal technique so remarkable in Robert Shaw's work, or Peggy Rizza's reliance on her own ambivalent sensibilities; it could be said, though, that what all these poems share is a desire to renovate tradition, to compel the recognition that, in Martin Walser's words, 'The metaphor of the "death of literature" comes an eternity too early; only when the objects and their names would melt into one, only then would literature be dead.'

James Atlas
Cambridge, Massachusetts
August, 1972

Alan Williamson

War in the Valley of Vision: Christmas 1967

One year, the papers were full of the triple conjunction
That might bring back the star of Bethlehem.
I lay on my stomach,
Arranging and rearranging the manger figures.
Mary's gown was the condensed blue of ozone,
Melchior's shoulders all ermine.
Then the golden tree warmed and sprouted
In the naked hand of the Child,
As the naked plug reached the socket . . .
A snow village receded in lights
To the heart of a blown, silvered bell.

Through the glass wall
Of a ninth-story Cambridge classroom, Christmas belongs
To street crews wiring six-point, badge-like stars.
To each point of their compass,
An on-off bulb, a wink of God,
Freezes in ever green,
The go-ahead.
Relief, then: to be drawn slowly through landscapes
Toward Christmas behind the thick brick
And branch-level windows
Fronding white stars in the mornings
Of Chicago, a Gay Nineties dream.

In the dim-out of lights in the chair car
The aisle joggles
With the suitcases of soldiers,
And the old woman reading the *New Testament
In Crossword Puzzles*, cackles
'Make way for one of our officers!
I feel so much for those boys . . .'

She rambles into family history:
'You haven't lived till you've had grandchildren,'
But her favorite story
Is the death of her first one,
And how He strengthened her
(The woman is ill: waiting His will,
She has refused an operation; in the dining car
She must eat her meal standing) . . . the rapt voice
Sinks, slushing with the train wheels,
Slowing time incredibly,
As Blake: 'at a tragic scene the soul drinks murder
& revenge,
& applauds its own holiness.'

I have said nothing. Her stringy
Eye-muscles flick my way. A town
Passes in a sheet of plate glass
With one stray seagull crossing
And black divider beams rising to meet it
Like bullets from the center. Twenty years
Are becoming two thousand . . . The earth we have turned to glass,

The outside of the Christmas bell: do we hear it tolling,
Hear our own scurries fading
Like old churchmice? All winter, the radical
Dinner parties intone the word 'Breakthrough'
To the oval click of wineglasses;
We fall in a stupor
Down the circles of the world,
Where the retrograde aeons of space
Come, like a point in the distance,
To the mother mantled with stars,
The king bowed down among ermines,
The unswaddled child
With the golden tree in his hand.

I'm up before my wife and, almost, before everyone:
Churchbells at lull; the girls across the hall
Playing Vivaldi . . .
The empty bottles slide into the bag with a musical neatness.
I try to keep my kaleidoscope head as even;
Memories, headaches slip, cut, shine.

Courtyards and backstreets sprawl out peacefully
As sunning mannequins . . . the paradise
Of younger summers, parties', girls' addresses.
How fast they blurred together, the unique
Scenes of my keyed-up blunders, freak successes,
My life-plot rearranging
Week to week, as dream to dream:
The violet tarpaper-brick, the sinking asphalt . . .
Then, Cambridge walked in a gin-blur
Was Cambridge:
One tree in a field of dust, each twig in flower . . .

And the mornings still weirdly merciful, a coolness
On half-folded wishes; not yet the hour
Of the shadows lifting, the shadowless roofedges angular
As a fate, the Satanic wings . . . No: time relents
Like music;
All the peaceful voices, all the telephones faintly whirring
Are for me, and I don't have to answer.
My hands give up their slight trembling.

Should I give up drinking? Shall I wake my wife?

Here, the whitest roses
Learn the lesson that life is fire: the secret glassblower
Distends their petals, bids the small veins run
Red miles.
In the calm upland air, the cypresses
Bend with the tensile
Throat-muscles of swans.

A place to go mad or sane: as, moving
Before the self-portrait in the *Jeu de Paume*,
One sees the centering eye
Break into its different focus,
A swirl of paint, the green blindness
Of fish muscle in unlighted sea.

A place with a calm good-bye
For the sufferer: lines framed from the ledger,
Monsieur Van Gogh est sorti guéri.

I feel the blunt legs
Of his bed reach down into the spinning,
The walls of his nights tighten
And press like a seed-pod to morning,
To days and the works thereof,

The works: the eye's never quite motiveless
Gift to the things of its death,
A breath taking in
And letting go
What is taken and goes, those stars
Shedding light in glass panes,
Cured, gone out,
Starting to die—

That earth flaring up, sun getting a chill—

Hello, goodbye.

Oh let's be big bears, and roll in the bed of the family
till midnight, reading the detective stories
where grandpa's sweet head turns up in a nightcap of blood,

and pull the fog in tighter around the house,
around the Grand Hotel like a big bronze Alp,
content with the world's guilt, and a slow fire . . .

We read high up in the storm, hearing the glass
peal around us like bells; when we went out,
fifteen trees were down in the *Hohematte*,

and they brought dogs to track through the roots in the air
for something—we couldn't tell, from the German—
but we liked the rain-bearded muzzles, and ate late at the Restaurant
  Schuh.

But we are good children, and always wake up believing
this is where we are purely happy. The air breathes thin;
the long red Swiss rugs lift up at the end, with a sigh.

The patterns are jewel-scale: flowers in the mountain
meadows where we wander all day, sweat and run
till we are happy, then decide it's all right to take pictures.

Knee-deep in goldenrod, trying to hold the good smile,
I hear two British children, invisible as crickets:
'How far shall we go?' 'Till we don't want to go any farther.'

And we would go there too; but the evening comes back, the
  mysteries,
the room where you lie, too cozy-red, a curl,
and I tiptoe out, not to hear my own complaining,

and hear it downstairs: the oldest, the family pettiness . . .
The Italian teen-ager, in cowgirl leather, surrounded,
gives me her eyes. And I am, miserably,

her conspirator, not in lust but
understanding. Mountaineering is the only answer.
'We had almost got to the blue knees of the Lady,

half-reclining all day, in her peignoir of ice and air,
when our bodies fell back through the several childhoods,
numbed at long tables, answered one look in four.'

I say, and the *minuterie* goes; skylight; blue stars;
feet liking the fuzz of the old treads, the return.

The car lights: carrying white candles at noon . . . 'I
Can't, till I know what it means,' my father said; when
I guessed, he said nothing and flicked the switch.
The West Side came at us, shellshocks of sunlight, gray
Shafts of bay windows rising empty as pillars
At Hue, at Persepolis . . . Englewood Station: indefinite
Spaces, a few quiet, aging Negroes propped
Like lead soldiers at the windowledges. Pressure
Moistened my eyeballs. We watched America's Mainline
Narrow, the sidings stacked like needles, switches
Sizzling in the distance. The train pulled in unannounced
With most of the blinds down. An albino Coast Guard
Who looked seventeen was playing the role of porter.
'You're real lucky we stopped at Englewood—they think
There'll be trouble. Was that your father waving? No,
Don't lift the shade.' He grinned at me, shy and happy
To be useful in his night, in the gunmetal belly
That jerked us into motion, helpless as shot.

Jonathan Galassi

Elaine in Edge City

Up above the city it has rained
and little droplets shimmer everywhere
as if there were angels in the air
waving their mica wings and starting fires.
I'm standing at the porch rail holding tight.
Out here the wind is strong and cold tonight.

The night is wet and cold and the cliffs fall
at least a thousand feet below my feet.
Down in the dark some loud suburban queen
has spread her gaudy phosphorescent rocks
on satin for as far as I can see.
And out beyond them somewhere is the sea.

They say the smog has covered up the bay.
If our ship comes in we'll never know.
But would it make a difference anyway?
Everyone keeps an eye on the horizon.
What's to wait for? What could she possibly bring?
Last time I counted we had everything.

I take the freeway and go wandering
down in the valley on the hunt for buys.
I find better bargains every day,
but everywhere it's the same merchandise,
the same tie-ups in the parking lot,
the same paying for what I've got.

Things disappear and other things appear.
Cobras in pairs predict a coming tremor.
Suddenly they're curled up in the drawers,
safe in the mountains where they can't be swallowed.
Locked in the car, I read and wait for rain.
When the weather lifts they're always gone.

Summers the fire horns keep going off
north of us in the hills. I watch the smoke
shift in layers on the heat and head
to sea. Below the haze whole miles burn black.
At night the hummocks glow like bedded coals.
I go out on the rocks for midnight strolls.

I listen to the ocean when the moon's
down and the house stops creaking in the wind,
and stillness moves in like another breeze
and faintly in the distance something breathes
like a baby. I'm inside a shell,
cradled in the rhythm of the whole

world turning, humming like the bass
on a radio playing down the hall.
I roll over and look down on the lights
steady below me, blinking as I blink.
I think I hear you breathing by the bay
under my hand, just steps away. I say,
come in.

Letters from Mexico

'Zinecantan
Saturday, July 23
Dear Everybody—

My "grandmother" is weaving in her dark room.
She tells stories, talks about her pains.
She's about eighty. She wants to know
why I'm not married.

Girls in the corners watch me sifting potsherds,
wonder why I can't weave or make tortillas,
I ask them in Tzotzil, "Do you know ten tongues?"
I am the strange one.

At five I watch the sunlight hit the mountain.
Heavy mists roll into the valley.
It rains. I stay in writing postcards. They say
I am at home here.

At the fiesta the girls wear ribbons.
The grandmothers laugh in the doorways and sell blankets.
Drunk men grab at my serape, making motions.
I know their language.

I have been learning how to weave from Grandma.
I've already finished my first blanket.
In my spare time I read or knit scarves.
I wear a nightie.

I have been dreaming of the revolution.
Down the valley I hear shots and horses.
Smoke from my fire billows under the flame,
mixes into the dark.

A sea of dark
or a sea of smoke
surrounds the fire. Under the acid
I smell the raw earth.'

I put myself into the hands of fate.
Nothing worked out very well.
I kept looking into the past for suggestions.
I knew my dreams meant something—
as a child I kept finding the perfect thing,
something like a ball of crushed paper.
It was more than that, but I had no clues.

The 24th Bobby is driving me to the airport.
The wedding's over, I'm flying back to my books.
At five we're stalled in front of Bellevue.
The Triboro is a river, tugboats end to end,
flowing out of gorgeous New York.
Wall Street is winking in the half light.
In this sunset anything is possible.

Rumors start spreading up the line.
Manhattan is sinking.
The bigshots are fleeing
into Queens, the anonymous, safe island.
The bridge is backed up for miles.
We put on our lights and peer into other cars.
Every one is packed with tycoons.
We roll down the windows and play word games with our
                                                  neighbors.

We beat them every time.
Old puzzles solve themselves out of thin air.
We can name all the Presidents in order.
Our desires are suddenly transparent.
We are open books with all the answers.
Life is simpler than we have been led to believe.
We revel in our discoveries and honk at the tycoons.
Now all we have to do
is put what we've learned into practice.

Then we notice the cars are moving backwards.
We're on a long conveyor belt carrying us back into the city.

Inside an hour we're in Manhattan.
It hasn't sunk. The streets are bursting.
Bigshots are bivouacing in the avenues, huddled in their coats.
We abandon our car.
No one offers us space on a parquet floor.
We lie down in the middle of Fifth Avenue and shiver all night.

In the morning the Sanitation Department puts things in order.
The cars have disappeared.
The bridges have been dismantled.
There is no way out of the city.
Helicopters drop care packages into our laps.
Later, we roam the streets like vandals.
Periodically the lights go out.
We get separated in the confusion.

I stand at the edge of the East River and gaze at Long Island.
It lies on the horizon like paradise.
I look up into the sky and forget what I knew.
My dreams are once again a mystery.
I tear up my ticket and throw it into the water.

Day and night we heard sound trucks and radios.
In their rumbling there was dissonance.
It stood for whatever you like:
it stood for the old war and the sinking dollar,
for the lapsed desire to become a government official,
for the inhabitants' fear of the city,
for the interminable personal and public *status quo*.
Above all it stood for the failure of mythology.
Relaxing became like driving in the Square:
nearly impossible in any direction.
We put on our headphones and listened to soothing sounds.
We got into bed.
In the morning we decided to drive north.
We drove straight north, stopping only for gas.
The traffic was discouraging: half the factories were on vacation.
But we were determined.
We took turns sleeping.
We exited onto the first appropriate two-lane highway.
It took us through charming coastal towns
with scenery and poverty.
We were intrigued by their picturesque qualities
but something drove us on.
The soil grew very sandy.
Houses were few and far between.
Only scrub pine survived in this terrain.
Finally we passed the tree line.
From here on, nothing but rocks and lichens.
It was chilly all day long. The night lasted four hours.
The only sign of civilization was an occasional
billboard advertising building materials.
At last they too fell away behind us.
It was us and the land.
We were exhausted but excited.
We looked straight into the sky.
The sun was about to go down on our left. The wind sounded quiet.
We stopped the car.

We were about to get out and enjoy the magnificent sunset
unimpeded by walls or vegetation.
The wind began to whirr and roar. There were other noises.
The light faded. We were afraid to leave the car.
We huddled together in the front seat.
We turned on the radio
and listened to mood music out of the south.

King Caesar's Windows

*The shipyards of Ezra 'King Caesar' Weston at Duxbury,
Massachusetts, were the greatest in America near the turn
of the 19th century.*

The Gurnet beacon shudders in the distance
off Powder Point, caught in the soughing wind.
King Caesar's windows keep their watch forever
over the empty water of the harbor.
Nothing moves except the brown sea reeds
bending the wind's way to the open east.

The blank black panes stare out on the flat east
as if a ship lay anchored in the distance,
hidden behind a thicket of sea reeds,
waiting for a favorable wind
to carry her into the shallow harbor
to dock among the pleasure boats forever.

King Caesar's crafty workmen were forever
building boats. The best fleet in the east,
some said the world, sailed out of his trim harbor
bent on some sweating seacoast in the distance
where a dark cargo waited in the wind
that shook their shackled bodies like thin reeds.

King Caesar stayed at home behind the reeds
watching his masts go up, the gold forever
growing in his countinghouse. The wind
smelled of his rumrunners from the east
carrying contraband, built to outdistance
challengers. At home they hugged the harbor.

King Caesar knew the currents of the harbor.
He learned the weather from the waving reeds.
From his front parlor he surveyed the distance
for his white sails, richer than Aegeus, forever
watching for sons returning from the east,
his pilgrim jaw set firm against the wind.

Now the thin windows rattle in the wind
and look out blindly on the glassy harbor,
expecting ships long lost to the wild east
to tie up suddenly among the reeds
and serve their master as they had forever.
Implacable they stare across the distance.

Dories knock in the distance. An east wind
fills the dark harbor. The brown sea reeds bend
before the windows as they have bent forever.

Paul Smyth

The farmer is dead,
Four sons went south from here
And never came back. A white bone lies
Beside the steps, and a red
Enamelled teapot. The day moon's sheer
Gentle persistence pries
Grey roofboards loose, and the iron bed
Despised by them now gone
Rusts on a lawn

Grown three feet high.
I know this house, I learned it
By nightmare's baffling rote: the squeak
Of leaning beams, the cry
Of anguished hinges, the scent and grit
Of plaster-dust in bleak
Dry dreamless rooms that flatly deny
The swamps of flesh and fear.
Now I am here.

Rank goldenrod
Has undermined the porch,
Grapevines loosen the shingles. First pride
Then passion failed. Spent pod,
Discarded trunk, extinguished torch—
This house once magnified
A young wife and the village God.
Now brash woodpeckers drill
The posts and sill.

I shoulder the doors
That open on broken walls
And curtains shredded on windowframes.
A hollow wind implores

My shadow, as it slides and stalls,
    To whisper the ruined names—
Their rooms, their tools, their meals and chores—
    My shadow, bent on the stair:
        Trespasser, heir.

> *Behold, I have refined thee, but not with silver;*
> *I have chosen thee in the furnace of affliction.*
> —*Isaiah*

I.

You stand alone.
A broken wall, pine trees
Drive roots beneath the bleaching stone.
The steady hissing of disease
Seeps from the ground. And these,
The fruits of moments Death has sown,
Death on his hands and knees
With chips of bone:

II.

You crouched in a cave of grapevines, knelt toward the hum,
The field of insects, watching the thick dusk spread
Like anguish over a face—you who had come
Running through swollen woods, who lied then fled
To this field's edge, this frantic hum the same
As thin internal humming that scorched not ears
But lungs and brain, that sizzling you would name
The Locusts. You knelt at the edge of seven years,

Then stood, and pushing aside the veil of vines
Stepped into the field: instantly all sound ceased—
Except, as it rose from the dead tree slowly on
Enormous wings over the murky pines,
The crow cawed twice. For a moment, all memory gone,
You wore the silks of silence like a priest.

III.

Always the threat,
Downstairs, of violence—
Whiskey and frothy shouting; yet
Silence was worse, the creaking silence.

And what was your offense?
Weakness: the kind that must beget
An iron obedience
Upon its debt.

Lying in bed
You heard his shouting rise
Around your name, a sound that led
To ruin, to facts like myths: his size,
His strength, his fists, his eyes.
You listened to the brook instead,
Its muddy compromise
Of hope and dread.

How to prepare?
You watched the ceiling, tried
To gauge his voice. Time was your lair,
And night, where hope and dread collide
Crushing the minutes. Outside
The brook kept gurgling, unaware
Of his terrific stride
Leveling the stair.

IV.

Like a pinball, shot and played against the slant:
roll down slip past two flippers clattering fall
into the trough but no so want to can't
green flippers red electric bumpers all
buzzing to touch and jingling on the board
back bending neon girls flash when they smile
now carom flee this bumper's cringing chord
upping the score clicked index of denial—

steel pinball chromeskinned shot electric effect
know nothing else not volts not any cause
so flipped and spinning monad o reflect
whirl neon girls hot face of him who plays
his nickel's worth of what? conceal steel's flaws
slick pinball chrome blushing with vivid praise.

V.

Now live with pain,
The god who flaps his way
Through sinew, joint, and wrinkled vein.
As close as breathing you obey
Pain's scraping beak by day,
By night his caw. Your bones disdain
The little prayers you weigh
Like suet or grain

But can't recite;
You think of a grinning skull,
Also a speechless thing, then bite
Your lip to make deep pain seem dull
Till sleep begins to pull,
To lure you in, till sleep seems right
And even masterful.
But in the night

Your nerves, that twist
Like roots down through your back,
Begin the ruttish whines that mist
Your eyes with turpentine and crack
Your skin—veins drip shellac,
Hot bubbling muscle-fibers kissed
To tar. Shrunk hard and black,
Your brain's a fist.

VI.

In the wavy bathroom mirror rippling lay
Five badge-like bruises: four finger-prints, the thumb.
He'd grabbed and held your throat like a fistful of clay.
Sick with pain and the smell of spilled Bay Rum
You winced touching those marks that seemed afloat
Like islands on your skin—his madness's map,
A clumsily worked projection of remote
Volcanic realms that would spread and overlap—

The blotch would be too hideous in school.
But the bus, your daily ark, could not be missed:
You readied yourself for playground ridicule
And washed your swollen face and buttoned your coat.
Then, in a last reflex of the will to resist,
You smeared your mother's makeup on your throat.

VII.

You knew so well
The fist that crushed your lip,
Had watched so closely as it fell
Or rushed in level from his hip,
That when that hand would grip
A chairback angrily you could tell
By a whitening knuckletip
Degrees of hell.

You braided strings
To divine your labor's wage:
The strands revealed that famine brings
A time of plenty, that every rage
Must, more or less, presage
Delight. You counted your breaths, logs' rings,
Making each thing the gauge
Of other things,

And thought you could
Store years themselves away
With little loss: you cut the firewood,
Each cord a year, the loss a day
In sawdust. But the ash was grey,
Buckets of ashes; and you understood
That life is the price you pay
For livelihood.

VIII.

Trudging across the field you could not say
The sum of corn, exhaustion, peas, and heat.

You lowered the buckets for the hundredth time that day
Into the shallow brook: *here two worlds meet:*
Over the stones and ooze of bottom slime
Flows water fat with life, with leafy plants
Whose white roots hold against the drag of time,
Resigned, resolved in undulating trance.

You looked deep in—past shiny browns and greens,
Past water and light and shadowy moving gloom,
Past metaphor: to one who kneels, who leans
Into the deepening breath, whose breathing slows—
Then turned, lifting the buckets, to resume
Soaking the twelfth of twenty dusty rows.

IX.

Why did you wait,
Shy, in the clearing? There
No question asked could compensate
For those unasked in shrill fear
Of sudden answers where
Death was a word. *It's getting late.*
You and the cooler air
Deliberate,

But still no word.
No voice responds here, none,
The woods keep silent. Now a bird
Questions the disappearing sun,
Bright edgy notes that run
Through heavy boughs. At dusk you heard
The air's long sigh begun,
A minor third

Raising the scent
Of withered grass and moss:
A dim hour paused, and bent
Slowly to gather up your loss,
The shadows cast across

Your lips with every breath, then went
    Into the pines that toss
        Bewilderment.

X.

You stand alone. A broken wall, pine trees
Drive roots into the sodden earth and drink.
Their boughs are dark with voices murmuring, 'Please'—
Mere statement, not a request. Your seasons shrink
And hissing fade like a long wave's foam and froth.
Four billion years ago parched cells first sipped
Nutrition from the steaming primordial broth
Defining life, and entering the crypt

Of age and place forever. Now, you wait.
The past backs off, the future turns and flees.
You arrange the shrivelled griefs, weigh what's left,
As a child will push cold peas around his plate.
Did those first cells drink to Charity or to Theft?
The pineboughs' ponderous tossing answers, 'Please.'

XI.

    Go back to the car,
        Give up this hopeless thing,
    Drive home. Wish on the blue-white star
    For simple moonlight, fields that sing,
        Declare that mornings bring
    New reasons, clear as the minutes are.
        Give up this hopeless thing.
            It's gone too far.

        Lying in bed,
            Imagine a chainlink fence
    With barbed-wire gates, a tin-roofed shed,
    Lean, iron-eyed guards who live in tents
            Nearby. For all time hence
    Let memories eat the meager bread
        Of despair, each violence
            Dying or dead.

How to prepare?
Fear rolls large flickering eyes,
Swings nimbly from rib to rib—'Beware!
Kill him, feed him, muffle his cries—
A stack of heartbeats tries
Buying that hunchback out of there,
But fear is pennywise
Screeching, 'The stair!'

XII.

You drive all night—a windshield wiper's arc,
The headlights' sprawl, and the ever-dying hiss
Of tires on wet asphalt. At dawn you park
And step from the car and stretch, embracing this:
Green picnic tables, trash cans, the silence of mist
Drifting among the trees, and beside the road
Two crows devouring flesh. Those years subsist
On your will to devise their final episode,

You cross wet grass toward where the dead thing lies.
The patient crows retreat to a nearby tree.
You kneel. It was a hound. His stomach is torn,
Neck twisted, mouth open howling silence. And his eyes,
Opaque and staring skyward: through them you see
That threat of which his abstract howls still warn.

Peggy Rizza

The Pilgrimage Church

That last of schoolgirl summers—oh, all guts and sweet
simplicity, I took Europe in a sturdy stride. Polite,
intense, grasping German grammar, my days a neat
balance . . . The mornings meant gardens in sunlight,
streudel and cream at eleven. Evenings, the medieval towns,
cafés suspended over the city. Boat sounds
floated over river and dock, the fog on the mellow
old castle—but I remember most often that drizzling night
we climbed the 14 stations, each Wagnerian statue telling
its damp prayer. Reciting in German, my brother grew congruent.
Affectionate, brilliant, he told me the meaning of botanical labelling.
In the darkening pilgrimage church he spoke
of the Hundred Years War and the forms of Baroque.

A Gatsby setting ten years later: rural, bored
by summer nights of crickets and secrets on the steps,
'Humoresque' and sitting on the running board of Daddy's Ford . . .
You never liked to talk about the details, and yet
somehow I know the smells of Grandma's house: gingerbread,
the cows, and the soap of new washed hands of men
in beaten denim—that was your father. You said
a restlessness would often seize you and then
no force could stop you. I imagine you alert,
audacious, a saucy pony of a girl; when I see
you middied at the beach in Charlestown skirts
in 1934, I wonder how could I not also be
in those chipped-corner snapshots captioned 'Arline.'
Weren't you my mother even at sixteen?

Charlotte

Sunblind, I can find
you only as an outline,
six years old, on one
of your final days.
Your death is why I grew up
thinking polio and worms were got
by sitting on wet ground.
Your mother found you
one June morning soon
after, a thin, grown
baby in gray knickers,
already too sick and weak to whine
'Mama, I don't want to go to school.'

This is the tree. Years
later, my mother set out
Grandpa's forbidden black
umbrella here, purchased 30 years before,
a farewell gift from Austria.
Kneeling beneath the black
tent, she spread her dolls about
with listless fervor,
wishing for a sister.

At 8 years old, I stood
beneath this tree, hiding
from the stable, dressed
in my itchy green riding pants,
terrified of horses.
Even then, what forces drew us
close, what feeling too secret and hard
to speak of?

Auntie, summers and Christmases,
birthdays and picnics have passed
at least sixty times between us.

Each was distinct in your
tight, perfect life.
But I'm old enough for
nonchalance, old enough to be your mother.
Lotte, what you never knew
has not hurt you.

I seem to pulse for water, urge for
arms as cool, as sleekly naked as an otter.
The trees are cast between my vast
suspended sky and sun. The clouds are moist and vast.
All memory, I press to cross a field of swaying goldenrod
and tiny ferns and mosses. Smooth long grasses nod
and lure me staring to the lake—fragrant, vaguely green,
persuasive. Suddenly I swim with clean
and unaccustomed strength, my shoulders fluid. Rushes
love my heavy hair. Charmed, the gorgeous
water bushes wave. By heart I know their pull, I darkly
feel their fishy grace. Their secret knowledge drags me
back and back. The promised peace, the past, the lake,
enticing, beds me down. Backstroking, I need never wake.

Storm over the Lake, Midsummer

For G.E.S.

Finally, that moist day of thick, salt
suspension, when all whirrings wound down,
when lights flickered a moment,
then emphatically, failed,
the rain, sudden and leaden,
approached like an air
force, thunder flushed out the
house, lightning advertised, 'watch me!'
But the sunset, so distant, pursued
its pink business,
ignored the dark
thunder, the ice
cuts of voltage,
the quick yellow rushers just
under the lake. The lake's
top layer of water, like
geese in November, swept
south.
The stir was soon over.
the deep peaceful lake
creatures, the otter
and muskrat, the rapid black
snapper, the bluegill and
pickerel, fathomed only a
premature darkness, and somewhere,
a vague interruption in
their fishy lives.
For us on land, no
duck rose
from the wild hedge, no god
signalled the last acts with
vast flashing light. Only
the canoe could be seen, filled
with water, and the branch
of a young
birch
that had died violently,
and the wing of an angel, posed as a
rainbow.

Dryburgh Abbey Garden

Once only nuns
kept these paths, tore
up the weed,
the wayward blade
of garlic grass, wore
unwashed woolsey
and sweated in the forenoons.

Soft flowers, frail
petals billowed gold and spilled
their pink onto the onion beds,
trespassed on chive and mint and bay.

Sometimes a duchess hushed
through these gardens
wearing green brocade.

Now, on the edge
of the grounds
of the garden
a woman in denim,
a part of the convent,
is feeding the horse and the cow
with amazement. Mystic,
she passes the cherry and plum
trees, the scourged branches ablaze
with mauve, blood and fuschia,
beside the mossy well.

Voyagers, vagrants, almost transgressors,
our hands
never felt of this soil.
Dazzled by our first
glance at heather and royal
blue petals, we thirst
for more breathtaking sights,
more color, more perfection.

Buoyant and sound
as a new young boat
the nun on the boat
crossing the island sound
leans on one elbow and
clearly, forgets
and as the boat parts
from its mooring in sudden
stopping sun, her one   /   abandoned hand
carelessly adjusts her nun's
underwear. Abrupt wind
takes the hair from her hat.
Smiling into the seagulls   /   serenely
she leans on the rail
the whole afternoon journey.
And come night, lulling into the vanishing
harbor, the varnished brown hulls
of the waiting boats
fading, she watches
while others flow onto the docking,
or rush to the families in their lighted homes.
She watches   /   the masts—
blue, green, vaporous yellow, brown—
above the waves like tocking
metronomes.

Concerned for my father again
after ten hostile years,
my mother anxiously craned over his bed,
strained to hear his whispers,
smoothed his ghostly hair. Sometimes
sitting stiff, looking child-like and humorous,
sucking his liquids through a straw,
he followed Mother's movements in the room,
surely sensing that . . . Soon
he grew too weak and submitted,
a hundred pounds, to having Mother
lift him from his difficult positions.
Contrary as ever, he surprised us
with his impotent bursts of temper.
The sunlight oppressing the wide-windowed room,
our anger, our pity, all annoyed us.
Other old men dying called deliriums,
ranted obscenely while tied to their beds.
But Father, somewhat sheepish, took his dying
quietly. Perverse, alert, he waited—
spotted, throbbing, hollow—
and looked our guilt straight in the eye,
threatening to last
and last . . . He rasped,
'How much will all this cost?'
Assembled like a posed family photograph, most
likely we remembered
those childhood staring games:
he could always win then, too.

James Martin

A Reunion

*The Cocoanut Grove nightclub burns
in Boston, Massachusetts, 492 perish.
November 28, 1942*

1.
It was bad.

In the kitchen,
people burned and drifted
in the flames
like pollen off a stalk.

I thought it was from grease
on the stoves.
I remember the cook gagging,
filling his eyes with ice.

We sat in the food freezer
until they found us.
Shivering.

I live with my sister.
She rubs this salve on my hands.
I don't need it, but she would be sad,
I think, to know they've healed.
We have our routines.

2.
I remember the air

got thick, like jelly
on my face;
it crawled in my dress,
a stood hotness.

I woke a burnt cow.
The third day, the graft
just slid off,
like an orange peel, on the floor.

I had no new skin.

One night one small girl
stepped in our ward by mistake.
She asked our names, bed by bed,
then, last, slowly, she held
her hand to my cheek
and left.
We all asked for mirrors the next day.

3.
All we had were drunken kids.
It just fell on them.

One man walked behind the bar
and poured himself a drink.

Sailors, dancers, everyone swallowed
some heat.
When they got out,
the cold was like a hot stone.
A girl fell, holding the door
for someone else.

There was a force, a power, loose
in there we never caught.
A gift to us,

for part of one minute,
everything we were, and would be,
stood before us, ready.

We were a child,
a family.

48

4.
You see this scar.

I just stood there
watching them go.

One hot man stood on
two dead women
to get at a window.
I tried to help a woman limping;
she kicked me.
I still toast the brothers
I found that night.

I sell insurance,
and all I know is, I
tell them where I got that scar.
They buy.

I. Pastor Bonhoeffer Becomes Engaged

Friend, I must tell you that she has entered my heart
  Like a bullet. During evening worship I find
My last prayers travelling without shame to a white
  House in Pätzig; I am still dreaming at curfew!
Her mother is torn by this, and I am great at
  Persuasion, but my future is uncertain now . . .

  'Maria, I write after four weeks in this cell
They have given me, better said, I was given *to*.
Stand firm. The reason for my presence here is well
Beyond discussion. Have you got your trousseau packed,
Or do women *pack* such things? I have heard them call
This prison healthy because we are exercised
Each day. They will censor this, but I am not blind,
Dearest, my only sweat has been from a cramped
                         leg.'

Now you should know of these stages.
The first is passive body. I
Must say you will be spit upon
For this, but spit cannot drown us.
Frankly, we are beyond that now.

The second is your point of view.
Ideologically, it is
Not ambidextrous, as each one
Of you will see. I will not lie
To you: these are the *safe* stages.

He is prone to shaking rages
And shaking hands. One cleverly
Died with the bombs taped to his arm.
You know that I am beyond this,
So these words are both harsh and true.

Your thoughts are a crime, or can be so
Construed. Stage four is preparedness:
You know of lives which must be hidden,
And you hide them. What more can be
Said? His past is not contagious.

And what is the last of these stages—
You know if you have talked with me
It cannot just be *said*. No one
Who wipes off spit is free in this,
Or has a perfect point of view.

IV. 'Your Führer is not AntiChrist . . .'

'Why so hard?' the charcoal once said to the diamond;
'for are we not close relations?'
Nietzsche

Bonhoeffer: I have no proof the difference
Is more than pills, or facial hair,
His peptic voice, the olid trance:

The German brain that holds me here
Is not insane. Is not insane
Or sane as mine which holds me here.

(But who has thought he is insane?)
Or finally seen no difference
In children held to kiss this man

And folly kissed? This man has sense.
And soldier, I should kiss this man,
And that has made the difference.

Soldier: You are his Christ in *Todesbanden*:
His Pastor of the Chains. It has
Been said you turn your bath to wine;

He keeps you here in hopes of this.
But *this* is not a Christian jest,
Or schoolroom joke, and never was.

Pastor, need I speak the rest?
You cannot wash your hands with wine,
Or wish to murder him who blessed

The church you met to burn us in.
I accuse you
Who are Jews of 'free' confession.

Bonhoeffer: I have no God to flex for you.
Your Führer is not the AntiChrist
Who, shall I say, has more to do—

Was Goethe's greatest sin at last,
Unfaithfulness? A battered wife?
Are sins of the sons uncursed?

We treat our fear of God in life
As secret wisdom. What shall we say
Then to those who fear *men*? And if

You ever preach of this, or me,
I would advise, Jeremiah,
Chapter 31, verse 3.

IX. *Pastor Bonhoeffer's Last Prayer, On The Importance Of Illusion*

Is unfinished.
It contains too much that is wise and good,
Unfinished, unfinished.
'I have just now finished Dostoievsky's
Memoirs from the House of the Dead.

It holds a great
Deal that is wise and good. I am thinking
About his assertion
That man cannot live without hope.' The world
Is unfinished and hope follows

Your illusion.
He knew that. He knew that illusion moved
Germans, before hope moved
Illusion. *Re*moved it. 'The danger here
Never lasts more than a few minutes.'

And we see him,
At least I see him, in the cell's air, tears
Welling, more slowly than
A tear wells loving us, his face so red
And welled, tears like string in his eyes,

Gasping for air,
More air, like ink, into his life. Because
He has kept on writing.
All this time, kept on writing about
The tear on my cheek, rolling.

Richard Tillinghast

One Poem Against History

The bears, rattlers, quicksand, savage
brambles, flash-floods and Indians
stood off the white frontier
nailing down its dominion over the earth.

What use do these ringed, streaked,
spotted and speckled cattle make
of the soil? Do they till it? Revelation
said to man—Thou shalt till the ground—
This alone is human life.

The animals, vulgarly called Indians
stumbling over the frozen earth,
the Creek nations crossing Arkansas
trailing thousands from border to border,
burying ten or twenty at each resting-place,
shepherded by rifles, wolf-packs,
flocking vultures . . . *A fact which to my mind*
seemed a lesson indeed to the American nation
is that they will not travel on the Sabbath—

these refugees in their flight to the Jordan
or the place where the sun sets,
on the run from the farms and jets
of the promised land.

Three of us in a motorboat
steering by full moon through foggy canals
cutting through sugar cane plantations

Fifty miles out of New Orlins
Cajun country, black cottonmouth moccasins
the length of a man in the bayou

Cajun trapper in a motorized pirogue
trapping muskrat, neutria, 'anything with fur'
$1.50 per hide in good condition

Two brothers named Robichaux
in a Dodge pickup, throwing ducks
to their cousins outside the hardware store

Marsh life waking in the dark:
gurgling, sneaking, murdering, whooping—
a muskrat breast-stroking through weeds towards food
frogs bellowing, bulbous water lilies adrift
cypresses digging their roots into water borne ooze
dark juices collapsing cell walls
oil rigs flaring thinly in daybreak

Light dawning in our hunting nerves—
eye-squint keener as we rose in the tippy pirogues
when the ducks set wing and glided down
shotguns deafening, slamming our shoulders.
We piled the boat between us with ducks
bloody swamp-juice sloshing our boots,
blood high with hunters' joy.

Until

I wanted to get you a picture of the room
where the two of them sat always
in the dimness of things: the windowseat clouded
by a shorted lamp, the samovar
thick with tea, outdated railway passes
catnip mouse, books piled against the nailed-up door—

Those were some of the things. One of them would strike
days off in bunches, always behind, remarking
'First day of winter,' 'President Harding
born, 1865.' The other one
would sometimes weep over the spectacle, and check
lists arranged for errands repeatedly begun.

Sometimes when water trembled in the drains
and drugs or lack of supper burned the world's dust away,
they saw things their way till the yellow day
and wandered the elated gardens. But mostly
the cat crumpled cellophane
and someone went down for groceries.

No mail came, no offers. Stories below, pedestrians
inched their way antlike through snow that fanned
the vague streetlights with a flutter and stabbing stroke.
No one came stamping through the door, up stairs
and trembling corridors to where
they sat smoking and dazzling the room with talk.

How many winter mornings waking wrongly
at three or four
my mind the only luminosity
in the darkened house . . .
Covered,
my wife richly breathes
her eyes turned deeply in
on dreams.

I am alert at once
and think of the cat
coasting on its muscles
from closet shelf to bureau
grave and all-seeing
caring not at all.

The face   the faces
waiting
toward ponds
empty-handed and with tenderness
hoping the hourly day might melt and flow
One could reach out—
there might be a daily salvation

Out the windows slowly
a dull light is covering the
world without end:
snow patches and mud ruts,
the neighbor warming up
his car.
The world refuses
to bless
or to be blessed.

In country churches sheaves of wheat are brought in.
Flowers are laid in the whitewashed sills of the deep windows.

As is decent,
the old and sick are taken driving in the country,
afghans and sweaters over their knees.
They praise the sunlight glowing about them through the glass.

Cottage gardens they have never seen before.
Sunflower stems sag helplessly beneath the enormous blossoms,
huge dahlias blur their eyes with unheard-of brilliance,
and even the late asters are not homely.

In their cities
people are glad for small favors.
They crowd the parks and spread out over the grass.
Or in an outdoor café, patient with a slow waiter.

A week of rain will kill it,
yet the kitchen-help and shop-girls are laughing
through the big square
going home from work in the rain.

They clack their umbrellas along the fence
of the closed amusement park,
and peer through at the rides and concessions.
The boarded windows of the dance pavilion highlight and gleam
like patent leather in the rain.

They see themselves inside still,
as they were,
faces glowing up from the new lagoon
floating beside the upside-down pagoda
and the ghostly painted paper lanterns.

The Fingers of One Hand

to Marcia

1.

I sit naked among the plants of the garden and
some of our own.
The sun opens our gradual
myriad pores—
skin of flower and man.
From the parts of me we share,
the glossy body-hair
tangled like beach grass
smoothed by wind   color of the sun,
my brown cock
as funky and road worn
as an old moccasin—
the two billion year old body!

Our varied natural smells,
mixture of juices
from the love of a night,
begin to rise from my sunny skin.
They haze over me   intermingled
with the moist earth smell
dewy long grass
the hardy, wax-skin vermilion flowers
that come out of the earth
with no human care
or human names.

From my hands I take the smell of Redwoods,
my thought takes its objects
the way a plum
takes the muscles you have
from tasting plums.
A few drops of dew
drift
from the loquat tree.
In its branches
is the daytime moon.

2.

To write you a poem—
for what does language
have to do with us?
I started with a phrase from Yeats,
'the labyrinth of another's being'
and now I wake
in the midst—
a cloud   a thicket of energy
where we sleep every night   for hours
suspended in the depths of ocean
or languidly reclined across the sky
like diagrams of our constellations—
while the moon sinks through
our western windows.

In the morning I wake   smiling
remembering   and forgetting
everything
in the diamond-blue of the sky
your sleepy laughter
the Japanese green of your eyes.

3.

For many nights
I was in love with
the black-blue tunnels   dark rainbows
hurtling projectile returning, returning
to its source in the in-going
on-going spirals—
and at the source
the shimmering skull.

In its place I begin to see
a picture of you—
Source of Light, we
are the Persian lovers
sitting as we do
on the low overhung bed

amid the brilliant mosses   and light-living ferns
hearing the stringed instruments
high on the California air
in the fragrant tops of Redwoods and Eucalyptus—
Both of us   like the Little Prince
on his wavy Persian rug
radiant   on the moon's bright edge.

4.
Yesterday   next week   that time in the forest
weren't we
creatures of the forest floor
dying   growing
between the sun and rotting debris—
on the forest floor and beneath
feet into dirt   or into air
using the inexhaustible sunlight
as it saps our energy
zaps us with life.

But life lives us!
The very dirt beneath our feet
is being lived
by tiny creatures—
a swarm of cell-fuck—
the trip was as it is
before our cells
joined it
as fuel and fire.
The trip was us before we were the trip.

Like K-SAN on the Bay Bridge
trying to jolt our car
with its message
of electric blues guitar—
Unknowing   or even knowing
we juice into a synapse
long splashes   spurts of energy
from the future a million years old
from the present into another life

(May these words come in
to the child's mind
next time around)

or into the imagining   vast mind
that gardens us
and glows through every leaf
each light-cell   breath-quick   heat-zap.

'Fled is that music'—
Forest murmurs   forest
answers and echoes   treetop
processions passing through
The Redwoods have grown
old   and they do not love death—
thick ribbed bark their suffering —
as our skin has turned
into our nerves.
We are already so old
our skin   the leather of our clothes
our words: Redwood bark.

5.
When our love shines   or branches out
like waves of light roaring   through air
without sound
I feel that we
are the yin-yang eggshell moon
swaying the tides of the world's oceans.
In a flow that can't be grasped
the tide goes out   comes in
rolling the pebbles   flattening the sand
in patterns of the shores
of clear-light continents so *there*
you can see right through them.

Robert B. Shaw

Janus

Wise tribe, the old Romans—
spiriting up an adequate
god to attend to every angle,
packing the Pantheon.
Take this old retainer, erected
where you would nowadays expect
a ticket booth or a hatrack:
patron alike of low posterns
and of exalted portals,
god of gateways, steady-lipped
genius of entrance and egress.

Pre-dating Peter
as keeper of the keys,
he carries a commanding bunch
in his left hand, a hefty staff
warningly in his right.
For a deity whose proper
feast falls on New Year's
he appears awfully sober,
even a trifle dull,
except for those alarming, double
features from the neck up.

Consider how he stood
at the City gate, one set
of eyes stiff on the lookout
for the foretold invader,
the other pair detailed to cover
possible subversives.
Or in the temple porch, he
marked a man's going out
even as his coming in.

Men slept easier
for this unfaltering vigilance—
odd as that may seem to us
who wince at supervision.
If he sees whatever passes,
that is reason ample enough
to kindle me to mistrust.
I wouldn't want, or stand to have him
darkening my own doorway—
tough-whiskered as Saturn,
cut from the same gray stone,
flinty-eared as midwinter,
two-faced as time.

Recessional

And we, too, have witnessed
empire put downhill.
Bristling in our own backyard,
vegetable tribes resist
the niceties of our will—
what the settling men found hard
to settle is hard still.

Seed released outruns the sower,
taking sway over the land;
tussock and the twig impede
the progress of the mower.
Beds we civilized by hand
reinstate the exiled weed,
soil behaves like sand.

Primal imps of the perverse
are garden gods, infusing vices
into the veins of all we grow.
Ripening melons turn for the worse,
set on never becoming slices.
Every wilfully ailing row
puts me in mind of winter prices.

And it puts me in mind of Cain,
feeling murderous in the field.
How could his or any garden
hope to avoid the Lord's disdain
in view of Eden's yield?
Cain wore his mark of pardon
even after his forehead healed;

and the heirs to his estate
differ intensely over its worth,
but they live the lives they earn.

Labor is their enduring trait,
bringing the proud towns to birth
that we abandon in our turn
to labor in the earth.

The Pause

Only a slow-growing forest, met with
in the warming cleft of summer,
would have hosted such a moment—
that is where we were.

No living owner's name
was posted where we came to earth.
Slivered seed-hulls, winter litter,
lay round like brown manna,

in the oval clearing abandoned
cones dried and ravelled to tinder.
Nearby a forking stream
swam over tracts of pebbles, they

were creviced and gray as pebbles
dug from the dark side of the moon.
How shall I say what happened?
Summer came to a standstill,

birds grew sober, limp air mingled
into the crowns of trees and put away
puffing, maybe for good.
The stream ran sudden as blood

but it was all that ran.
Even our fates stood off awhile,
tireless, but disengaged,
broadly considering us the way

we might look at children tranced in play.
Cool eyes fanned over us, like leaf-shadows.
Halfway up the pines sunlight
may have played, for all I know,

in needles, priming the points—but
by then our eyes were shut.

In Witness

for Robert Fitzgerald

My way lay through a wood.
Under a guise of trees
all my old familiars stood,
off limits by law.
I recognized the species
of every one I saw,

even despite the lack
of leaves on all that lumber.
Now that I was back
I dropped my old esteem
and sought amid their number
a remnant to redeem.

I snapped a twig or two
to make a test,
and saw the blood flow
from the wormy bark.
I wandered west,
trailed after by the dark.

Gathering branches here and there
I could dream that I was led
by the Harrower
of the waste, wild land
who went harvesting the dead
with no hook but a hand.

One twig was sound and green—
that one I would keep.
I came to a clearing then,
round, empty and as good
as any place to sleep.
There I dumped my dead wood

and kindled it to fire,
the better to banish fear.

But as the flame grew higher
my single green twig cried,
'Lord, if you had been here
my brothers had not died.'

That morning tide, that upswing of the air,
wages against the wing of the house I lie in;
tuning now to its waves, my curtain rings
clink like a bustling housekeeper's bunch of keys.
Sleepers, awake: for doors and stairs are creaking musically,
skirling as though the entire house
were stretching in the sun,
letting the dew steam off its chalky shingles.
Linen quivers; a warm, barny smell
rides in at the window. Light is taking sway:

the firmament of shadow overhead
sifts out of the room, revealing
unmysterious ceiling. Square and white,
its four corners boast no dangling spies.
Once again I dreamt of dead relations,
Grandmother in the garden, another summer,
pinching a done flower from its stem,
yesterday's day-lily.
Handing it to me absently, passing on
—into what hidden place? No protocol
governs these wordless meetings.

So often now I'm strange to my own skin.
I could be standing there at the door—
not now, but twenty years from now—
taking this in, from the sun's first
foothold, a thin, quaking beam
where pinhead seraphs conjured out of dust
exult and swarm. And see, my heavier
self lies long and motionless in bed,
grown a sounder sleeper, guessing nothing at all,
till the light widens, and the wind
blows the white curtains in.

More grandly than a camel kneeling down
in desert twilight she assumed her place,
motioning me to join her at her right.
Spooky, I thought, this dining in state for two,
at one corner of a table built for twelve.
Her hand lay on the table like pressed wax,
the bones too easily seen, but beautiful.
A prism hung to the cord of a window blind
sprinkled a bracelet of rainbow on her wrist.
December; and the light was dropping off early,
but even in winter dusk her silver showed
the chastened glow of a century's polishing.
I puzzled over the function of my forks,
abashed by the graying, apron-clad retainer
shuffling toward me with a plate of soup.
The last remaining help, unused to company.
Most of the talk has left me. Only a few
sentences I remember, each one prefaced
by an apologetic almost-cough.
'Literary men now are no longer what
they were in my day, in my father's day.
My father used to see James Russell Lowell
walking on Brattle Street in his English suits.
You know that he was our Ambassador.
I don't suppose we've had a poet since
presentable enough for such an office.
Well, poets may be better unpresentable. . . .'
I mused over the room we just had left
and would return to; utterly insufficient
fireplace, sooty portraits, sets of Scott
and Trollope, obvious volumes read to pieces.
Fur of her three cats tufted the furniture. . . .
I made my answers while the rainbow band
retreated down the table from us, flashed
at last on the far panelling; when I looked
again, was gone entirely. Shadow filled

the air like a fine ash: suddenly even she
began to feel it. So she called out, 'Emily!
If you please! The lights!' (No guest of hers
rose from her table to approach a light-switch.)
Again the gray lady entered, touched the wall,
illumining us, and turned to take our dishes.
I saw their faces side by side for an instant
under the good light. Sisters they might have been.

Jane Shore

Mud Season: Vermont

Under us the white roads dissolve.
The car dives deeper into fog.
Avoiding me, your eyes are headlights.
They stab the growing dark. I am afraid
to touch you. We pass a barn collapsed.
A fat moon floods the yard. Nothing
can shatter this composure your face
wears like a frosted windshield. Tense
since we argued. Around us slushy fields
split open, sea-beds, one deer stunned.
When you reach suddenly for me
somewhere inside me an iceberg cracks,
some deeper anger hardens.
Spring is here, breaking up within.

The Lifeguard

The children vault the giant carpet roll
of waves, with sharp cries swing legs
wide over water. A garden of umbrellas
blooms down the stretch of beach. Far
offshore, always I can spot that same
pale thumbprint of a face going under,
grown bigger as I approach, the one arm circling
locking rigid around my neck. The other
as its fist hooks and jabs my head away.
Ear to the conch, ear to the pillow,
beneath a canopy of bathers each night
I hear the voice and pry the jaws apart,
choke on the tangle of sable hair that blurs
the dead girl's mouth: that anarchy
of breath dog-soft and still at my neck.
She calls from the water glass I drink from.
From my own throat when I swallow.

Somebody said the sea would come to us
cutting like an army through wheat—
its captive women, dolphins in the wake
of our little boat. As water drains
every wife's a sea-wife. Such traffic
you would think it market day.
Hooked to their elbows, baskets
of apricots and limes
anchor the widows in the muddy slopes
where the world begins. The elements
have never been more married.

I have grown to love tending this garden
that barks and coos in the moonlight
when there is a moon.
Spindly giraffes cluster at the bow.
Ants inch down the plank in twos.
The sheep are nervous. Their thick wool
steams as the dew burns off.

Crises crush men more. In sleep
my husband's pitchy hands hammer the air
as if another boat could float us back
to who we were. I imagine
I am the mountain he teeters on
as every wave of wind comes past.
I watch for clouds.

Landing off Season

Jetties extend sturdy gangplanks
to the rows of evacuated bungalows
the rigid gulls coast over. In the wake
of another winter tracing your yard,
one skimpy hedge. This season's siege
is on. The porch light makes all the blues
green, the greens blue, your skin
yellowish. Your fingers have a weave
where you press the kitchen screen.
All afternoon the propped sweet
potato sprawled from the cloudy glass
you toyed with, and in the level darkness
I could see how privacy was torture,
my visit, a kind disruption of trees
in tall grass. Now we joke, dismantling
a lobster. The butter grits.
I can locate isolation on any map.
Everywhere I step is a staircase
to sabotage. You will know. When I survive,
this leaf, here, bends toward light.

Emily Dickinson

In the household of my brain
nine ladies
sit, old tenants gossiping
over wash. I'm used to

their tricks, how
a glass of water
held to the sun makes
a prism in my palm

in my palm, in my palm
the fabric
of Joseph's coat, stolen
from the atmosphere.

Living in this nunnery
of one, I age
gracefully, unlike women
whose earlobes stretch
heavy with antiques.
I have grown so
thin, my cheeks a fine
bone china, even my teeth hardly
shut out light.
Striped, dyed, color-
fast prints I swaddled in
I switch for my severe white
habit

habit of eggshell, pulp
of the apple, coffin
satin; habit of hot
stars, the quick
of the nail, the pages
of my lexicon.

Even my dog Carlo
rolls up his eyes
as if the ladies, those
passionate ladies
splash their paints
onto my patchwork
quilt of white, blinding
the eye that colors it.

Dieting

Always I am full of numbers,
the sad arithmetic of my body.
Every morning I weigh my feelings in
like a heavyweight champion,
wishing my robe were satin
with my name stitched on back.
Oh I am an enormous harbor.
Fear is in the breeze.

Where do the ounces of fat go? To China?
This is how the Christmas turkey feels
as the white meat is carved from him.
This is the loneliness of the last tooth
in the gum-plateau
when you are hungry
and the body comes on with all the commotion
of The Industrial Revolution.

This is how the skinny madonna felt
as she shies away from the angel
in Martini's 'Annunciation'.
The room is full of terrible surprises
each time you walk in.
Sometimes the strangers have wings.
They're always wanting you to do them a favor.

I have never eaten at the celestial Maxims
and so escaped the embarrassment of not knowing
which fork to use.
Instead, I am sinking into your three hundred dollar mattress,
that fleecy hunk of white bread.
Remember when we ate our way through Italy?
My hair fanned out like spaghetti on the pillow
and the pensione smelled garlic under the sheets.

Frank said: That line kind of derails me.
Then in the attic he discovered a tangerine-leak.

I have always wanted to fall for a nomad
and be swept away like a tent.
Or be folded up neat as an altarpiece.
If only you could look at me that way!
From all sides! Cherubs dangling
from wire hangers in a soup-bowl full of clouds.

All the suitcases spilled from their racks
when the train lurched near Nice.
Our heads hurt! You said:
Words are such spies. Let's eat a ham sandwich.

Oh, hot apple of my eye,
all through dinner I was starved for you!
I want to swallow your colors whole,
your ivories and lapis lazulis,
the way the sea does, the way the blind do.
I love the lime look your eyes have
this early in the morning.
You taste better than all the fresh fruit cocktails
in the world, better than the bunch of radishes
that hang in the still-life over your bed,
better than the bronze Poseidon in Athens
which the museum guards would not let me taste,
but if I did, it would taste salty,
collecting the sea for so many centuries.

Am I a cannibal?
Eating little, I digest myself.
Meanwhile, Dawn is breaking over Boston,
Her rosy fingers curled like shrimp.
Picasso's omelette is singing on my plate.

Frank Bidart

To My Father

I walked into the room.
There were objects in the room. I thought I needed nothing
from them. They began to speak,
but the words were unintelligible, a painful cacophony . . .
Then I realized they were saying
                                    the name
of the man who had chosen them, owned them,
ordered, arranged them, their deceased cause,
the secret pattern that made these things order.
I strained to hear: but
the sound remained unintelligible . . .
senselessly getting louder, urgent, deafening.

Hands over my ears, at last I knew
                                    they would remain
inarticulate; your name was not in my language.

He's *still* young—; thirty, but looks younger—
or does he? . . . In the eyes and cheeks, tonight,
turning in the mirror, he saw his mother,—
puffy; angry; bewildered . . . Many nights
now, when he stares there, he gets angry:—
something *unfulfilled* there, something dead
to what he once thought he surely could be—
Now, just the glamour of habits . . .

                                    Once, instead,
he thought insight would remake him, he'd reach
—what? The thrill, the exhilaration
unravelling disaster, that seemed to teach
necessary knowledge . . . became just jargon.

Sick of being decent, he craves another
crash. What *reaches* him except disaster?

'When I hit her on the head, it was good,

and then I did it to her a couple of times,—
but it was funny,—afterwards,
it was as if somebody else did it . . .

Everything flat, without sharpness, richness or line.

Still, I liked to drive past the woods where she lay,
tell the old lady and the kids I had to take a piss,
hop out and do it to her . . .

The whole buggy of them waiting for me
                                      made me feel good;
but still, just like I knew all along,
                          she didn't move.

When the body got too discomposed,
I'd just jack off, letting it fall on her . . .

—It sounds crazy, but I tell you
sometimes it was *beautiful*—; I don't know how
to say it, but for a minute, *everything* was possible—;
and then,
then,—
       well, like I said, she didn't move: and I saw,
under me, a little girl was just lying there in the mud:

and I knew I couldn't have done that,—
somebody *else* had to have done that,—

standing above her there,
                    in those ordinary, shitty leaves . . .

—One time, I went to see Dad in a motel where he was
staying with a woman; but she was gone;

you could smell the wine in the air; and he started,
real embarrassing, to cry . . .
                              He was still a little drunk,
and asked me to forgive him for
all he hadn't done—; but, What the shit?
Who would have wanted to stay with Mom? with bastards
not even his own kids?

                    I got in the truck, and started to drive,
. and saw a little girl—
who I picked up, hit on the head, and
screwed, and screwed, and screwed, and screwed, then

buried,
        in the garden of the motel . . .

—You see, ever since I was a kid I wanted
to *feel* things make sense: I remember

looking out the window of my room back home,—
and being almost suffocated by the asphalt;
and grass; and trees; and glass;
just *there*, just *there*, doing nothing!
not saying anything! filling me up—
but also being a wall; dead, and stopping me;
—how I wanted to see beneath it, cut

beneath it, and make it
somehow, come alive . . .

                    The salt of the earth;
Mom once said, "Man's spunk is the salt of the earth . . ."

—That night, at that Twenty-nine Palms Motel
I had passed a million times on the road, everything

fit together; was alright;
it seemed like
              everything *had* to be there, like I had spent years
trying, and at last finally finished drawing this
                              huge circle . . .

—But then, suddenly I knew
somebody *else* did it, some bastard
had hurt a little girl—; the motel
                              I could see again, it had been
itself all the time, a lousy
pile of bricks, plaster, that didn't seem to
have to be there,—but *was*, just by chance . . .

—Once, on the farm, when I was a kid,
I was screwing a goat; and the rope around his neck
when he tried to get away
pulled tight;—and just when I came,
he *died* . . .
                    I came back the next day; jacked off over his body;
but it didn't do any good . . .

Mom once said:
"Man's spunk is the salt of the earth, and grows kids."

I tried so hard to come; more *pain* than anything else;
but didn't do any good . . .

—About six months ago, I heard Dad remarried,
so I drove over to Connecticut to see him and see
if he was happy.
                    She was twenty-five years younger than him:
she had lots of little kids, and I don't know why,
I felt shaky . . .

                    I stopped in front of the address; and
snuck up to the window to look in . . .
                              —There he was, a kid
six months old on his lap, laughing
and bouncing the kid, happy in his old age
to play the papa after years of sleeping around,—
it twisted me up . . .
                              To think that what he wouldn't give me,
                              he *wanted* to give them . . .

       I could have killed the bastard . . .

—Naturally, I just got right back in the car,
and believe me, was determined, determined,
to head straight for home . . .

                     but the more I drove,
I kept thinking about getting a girl,
and the more I thought I shouldn't do it,
the more I had to—

             I saw her coming out of the movies,
saw she was alone, and
kept circling the blocks as she walked along them,
saying, "You're going to leave her alone."
"You're going to leave her alone."

                 —The woods were scary!
As the seasons changed, and you saw more and more
of the skull show through, the nights became clearer,
and the buds,—erect, like nipples . . .

—But then, one night,
nothing *worked* . . .
            Nothing in the sky
would blur like I wanted it to;
and I couldn't, *couldn't,*

get it to seem to me
that somebody *else* did it . . .

I tried, and tried, but there was just me there,
and her, and the sharp trees
saying, "That's you standing there.
                   You're . . .
                      just you."

           I hope I fry.

—Hell came when I saw
         MYSELF . . .
               and couldn't stand
what I see . . .'

John Koethe

Bird

What bird has read *all* the books?
The crow lives by a passionate insincerity
That means naturalness in an impossible world

And so is a unit by which we can measure ourselves
In the real one. The swallow defines 'exact place'
So that we know it exists beyond sight

And the criminal depth of the night sky.
Yet owls never move, flamingos just
Stand there, victims of the tall trees

And emblems of space or beautiful hair.
Our little canary recalls the first crisis:
Inclined planes, the separate enterprises

Necessary if we are able to exist at all.
The birds cannot reach us.
But we hear the sleeping art of their music

And it hints at all the evaporated experience
We need for our simplest move, our first
Aspiration, 'flight'. Hummingbirds are just space.

Orange is the hue of modernity.
Greater than gold, shaky and poetic,
Our century's art has been a gentle surrender
To this color's nonchalant 'stance'

Towards hunger and the unknown, and its boldness:
For it has replaced us as the subject of the unknown.
We still like the same things, but today we handle them differently.
Among the signs of occupation in this contemporary war

The twelve identical corduroy suits of Erik Satie
Locate importance in repetition, where it really belongs,
There in the dark, among the lessons that sleep excludes.
I want to emphasize the contribution of each one of us

To a society which has held us back but which has
Allowed love to flourish in this age like a song.
Unable to understand very much,
But prepared to isolate things in a personal way,

The acres of orange paint are a sign
Of the machine that powers our amateur hearts.
The technical has been driven back
By river stages, exposing a vacant lot

Strewn with these tools, food and clothing
Awaiting the invention of limited strength.
We could begin selling ourselves, but the overture
Brings no response and the connection remains unsketched.

I can see there has been no change.
The body's a form of remote control
And its success is too exact to assist us.
Responding to the ulterior commandment

So much has failed in the abstract.
The phallus hid in the school bell
While the difficult fluid rose in the night.
In the apartment wild horses took you away.

The Friendly Animals

I see that my 'voyage of discovery'
Was only a method of continuous sleep.
I have suddenly noticed the vacant chaos
And the mysterious luck that has let me live
Among friendly animals and the other vermin
Who carried knives, short pieces of rope,
Hideous lampshades, cartons of pots and pans
To show me that whatever enters your life
Independently can be put to use later
When there is space in the cabin.

What did their purpose conceal
If not the simplest units of friendship?
Like a ship returning in a foreign language
They have turned into beasts, conscious only
Of one another, blind to perfection,
Finding peace only in each other's arms.

Domes

for John Godfrey

I. ANIMALS

Carved—indicated, actually—from solid
Blocks of wood, the copper-, cream-, and chocolate-colored
Cows we bought in Salzburg form a tiny herd.
    And in Dr. Gachet's etching, six
Or seven universal poses are assumed by cats.

Misery, hypocrisy, greed: a dying
Mouse, a cat, and a flock of puzzled blackbirds wearing
Uniforms and frock coats exhibit these traits.
    Formally outlasting the motive
Of their creation with a poetry at once too vague

And too precise to do anything with but
Worship, they seem to have just blundered into our lives
By accident, completely comprehending
    Everything we find so disturbing
About them; but they never speak. They never even move

From the positions in which Grandville or some
Anonymous movie-poster artist has left them,
A sort of ghostly wolf, a lizard, an ape
    And a huge dog. And their eyes, looking
At nothing, manage to see everything invisible

To ours, even with all the time in the world
To see everything we think we have to see. And tell
Of this in the only way we really can:
    With a remark as mild as the air
In which it is to be left hanging; or a stiff scream,

Folded like a sheet of paper over all
The horrible memories of everything we were
Going to have. That vanished before our eyes
    As we woke up to nothing but these,
Our words, poor animals whose home is in another world.

2. Summer Home

Tiny outbursts of sunlight play
On the tips of waves that look like tacks
Strewn upon the surface of the bay.
Up the coast the water backs up
Behind a lofty, wooded island. Here,
According to photographs, it is less
Turbulent and blue; but much clearer.
It seems to exercise the sunlight less
Reflecting it, allowing beaten silver sheets
To roam like water across a kitchen floor.
Having begun gradually, the gravel beach
Ends abruptly in the forest on the shore.

Looked at from a distance, the forest seems
Haunted. But safe within its narrow room
Its light is innocent and green, as though
Emerging from another dream of diminution
We found ourselves of normal, human size,
Attempting to touch the leaves above our heads.
Why couldn't we have spent our summers here,
Surrounded and growing up again? Or perhaps
Arrive here late at night by car, much later
In life? If only heaven were not too near
For such sadness. And not within this world
Which heaven has finally made clear.

Green lichen fastened to a blue rock
Like a map of the spot; cobwebs crowded with stars
Of water; battalions of small white flowers.
Such clarity, unrelieved except by our
Delight and daily acquiescence in it,
Presumably the effect of a natural setting
Like this one, with all its expectations of ecstasy
And peace, demands a future of forgetting
Everything that sustains it: the dead leaves

Of winter; the new leaves of spring which summer burns
Into different kinds of happiness; for these,
When autumn drops its tear upon them, turn.

3. DOMES

'Pleased in proportion to the truth
Depicted by means of familiar images.' That
One was dazed; the other I left in a forest
Surrounded by giant, sobering pines.
For I had to abandon those lives.
Their burden of living had become
Mine and it was like dying: alone,
Huddled under the cold blue dome of the stars,
Still fighting what died and so close to myself I could not even see.
I kept trying to look at myself. It was like looking into the sun and I
                                        went blind.

O to break open that inert light
Like a stone and let the vision slowly sink down
Into the texture of things, like a comb flowing through dark,
Heavy hair; and to continue to be affected much later.
I was getting so tired of that excuse: refusing love
Until it might become so closely mated to its birth in
Acts and words of love; until a soft monstrosity of song
Might fuse these moments of affection with a dream of home;
The cold, prolonged proximity of God long after night
Has come and only starlight trickles through the dome;

And yet I only wanted to be happy.
I wanted rest and innocence; a place
Where I could hide each secret fear by blessing it,
By letting it survive inside those faces I could never understand,
Love, or bear to leave. Because I wanted peace, bruised with prayer
I tried to crawl inside the heavy, slaughtered hands of love
And never move. And then I felt the wound unfold inside me
Like a stab of paradise: explode: and then at last
Exhausted, heal into pain. And that was happiness:
A dream whose ending never ends, a vein

Of blood, a hollow entity
Consumed by consummation, bleeding so.
In the sky our eyes ascend to as they sweep
Upward into emptiness, the angels sing their listless
Lullabies and children wake up glistening with screams
They left asleep; and the dead are dead. The wounded worship death
And live a little while in love; and then are gone.
Inside the dome the stars assume the outlines of their lives:
Until we know, until we come to recognize as ours,
Those other lives that live within us as our own.